THE DIGITAL METAMORPHOSIS

The Digital Metamorphosis

DAKOTA FRANDSEN

First Printing, 2025

The Digital Metamorphosis

A Psychological Analysis of Social Media's Influence on Introverted Individuals and Pathways to Radicalization

Executive Summary

This comprehensive psychological analysis examines the transformative effects of social media followings on previously introverted and socially awkward individuals, with particular emphasis on ego inflation, personality reconstruction, and the concerning pathway toward radicalization. Drawing from contemporary psychological research, case studies, and behavioral analysis, this report explores how digital validation mechanisms can fundamentally alter self-perception, social behavior, and in extreme cases, contribute to radicalization processes that have preceded acts of violence.

Abstract

Social media platforms have created unprecedented opportunities for social recognition and validation, particularly affecting individuals who previously experienced social marginalization. This report analyzes the psychological mechanisms through which introverted, socially awkward individuals undergo personality transformations when acquiring online followings. We examine the neuropsychological basis of social validation, the development of narcissistic traits, the formation of parasocial relationships, and the darker trajectory toward echo chamber radicalization. The analysis incorporates perspectives from social psychology, neuroscience, clinical psychology, and terrorism studies to provide a multidimensional understanding of this contemporary phenomenon.

Keywords: social media psychology, introversion, narcissism, ego inflation, online validation, radicalization, social isolation, extremism, parasocial relationships, digital identity

---

1. Introduction

1.1 THE SOCIAL MEDIA REVOLUTION AND IDENTITY FORMATION

The advent of social media platforms has fundamentally restructured human social interaction and self-concept formation. For the first time in human history, individuals can broadcast their thoughts, experiences, and identities to potentially unlimited audiences, receiving immediate quantifiable feedback through likes, shares, comments, and follower counts.

This transformation has proven particularly significant for individuals who previously struggled with face-to-face social interaction.

Traditional social hierarchies, which once relegated introverted or socially awkward individuals to the periphery of social networks, have been disrupted by digital platforms that reward different skill sets. Carefully curated content, edited communication, and the absence of real-time social pressure have created environments where previously marginalized individuals can thrive, accumulate social capital, and experience validation that eluded them in physical spaces.

1.2 THE PSYCHOLOGICAL LANDSCAPE OF THE INTROVERTED INDIVIDUAL

Introversion, characterized by a preference for solitary activities, deep rather than broad social connections, and energy depletion from extensive social interaction, represents a stable personality trait affecting approximately 25-40% of the population. When combined with social awkwardness—difficulty reading social cues, anxiety in social situations, and challenges with spontaneous interaction—individuals often develop negative self-schemas rooted in repeated experiences of social rejection or invisibility.

These individuals frequently internalize narratives of inadequacy, developing what psychologists term "rejection sensitivity"—a heightened awareness and anticipation of social rejection. This psychological profile creates particular vulnerability to the validation mechanisms inherent in social media platforms.

1.3 SCOPE AND OBJECTIVES

This report examines:

1. The psychological mechanisms underlying personality transformation in response to social media validation
2. The neurobiological basis of social reward processing and addiction
3. The development of inflated self-perception and narcissistic traits
4. The role of echo chambers in reinforcing distorted self-concepts
5. The pathway from social isolation to online radicalization
6. Case studies of individuals whose online presence preceded violent extremism
7. Intervention strategies and protective factors

---

2. Theoretical Framework: Understanding the Transformation

2.1 SOCIAL VALIDATION THEORY AND THE FUNDAMENTAL HUMAN NEED FOR BELONGING

Abraham Maslow's hierarchy of needs positions belonging and esteem as fundamental human motivations, superseded only by physiological and safety needs. For individuals who have experienced chronic social marginalization, these needs remain chronically unmet, creating what psychologists describe as "social hunger"—a state of deprivation analogous to physical hunger.

Social media platforms exploit this hunger through carefully engineered feedback mechanisms. Every like, comment, share, and new follower triggers dopaminergic reward pathways in the brain, creating reinforcement schedules that can become addictive. For previously marginalized individuals, this represents their first sustained experience of social validation, creating powerful psychological dependencies.

2.2 THE SELF-PRESENTATION THEORY IN DIGITAL CONTEXTS

Erving Goffman's dramaturgical theory posits that individuals constantly engage in impression management, presenting different "selves" in different contexts. Social media radically extends this capability, allowing individuals to meticulously construct, edit, and curate their presented identity.

Unlike face-to-face interaction, which requires real-time social processing and reveals authentic emotional states through microexpressions and body language, digital platforms permit careful construction of an idealized self. Introverted individuals, who often excel at written communication and thoughtful reflection, can leverage these strengths while avoiding their weaknesses in spontaneous social interaction.

This creates a feedback loop: the curated self receives validation, reinforcing the performance, which becomes increasingly divorced from the individual's offline identity. Over time, the gap between the online persona and offline reality can create cognitive dissonance, often resolved by devaluing offline relationships and experiences while increasingly investing in the digital identity.

2.3 PARASOCIAL RELATIONSHIPS AND FOLLOWER DYNAMICS

Parasocial relationships—one-sided relationships where one party invests emotional energy, interest, and time while the other party is unaware of the individual's existence—traditionally described celebrity-fan dynamics. Social media has democratized this phenomenon, allowing micro-influencers and ordinary individuals to accumulate followers who feel personally connected to them.

For the content creator, followers represent quantifiable social proof of worth and influence. However, the relationship remains fundamentally asymmetric and transactional. Followers consume content and provide validation, but rarely offer the reciprocal emotional support characteristic of genuine friendship. This creates a paradox: individuals can feel simultaneously connected (through follower counts) and profoundly isolated (through lack of authentic intimacy).

2.4 THE NEUROSCIENCE OF SOCIAL REWARD AND ADDICTION

Neuroimaging studies have revealed that social validation activates the ventral striatum, the same reward circuitry activated by food, sex, and drugs. When an individual receives likes or positive comments, the brain releases dopamine, creating pleasurable sensations that reinforce the behavior that generated the reward.

For individuals with histories of social rejection, this reward is particularly potent. Their baseline dopaminergic tone may be lower due to chronic stress and social deprivation, making the dopamine spike from social validation disproportionately reinforcing. This creates vulnerability to behavioral addiction, with individuals compulsively checking notifications, posting content, and seeking validation in patterns indistinguishable from substance addiction.

The variable ratio reinforcement schedule—where rewards (likes, comments) are unpredictable in timing and magnitude—is the most resistant to extinction. This is the same schedule used in gambling machines. Users cannot predict when their post will "go viral" or receive unexpected engagement, maintaining constant engagement with the platform.

---

3. The Transformation Process: From Invisibility to Influence

3.1 STAGE ONE: INITIAL DISCOVERY AND VALIDATION

The transformation typically begins when an introverted or socially awkward individual receives unexpected positive feedback on social media. This might occur through:

- A comment or post that receives viral engagement
- Accumulation of followers interested in niche content
- Recognition for expertise, humor, creativity, or appearance
- Validation from strangers in online communities

For individuals unaccustomed to social recognition, this initial validation creates profound psychological impact. Neurologically, their brain's reward system, previously understimulated, experiences intense activation. Psychologically, they receive evidence contradicting their negative self-schema—perhaps they are interesting, attractive, talented, or worthy of attention.

This stage is characterized by excitement, surprise, and cautious optimism. The individual typically increases their posting frequency, experimenting with content to replicate the positive response.

3.2 STAGE TWO: IDENTITY INVESTMENT AND BEHAVIORAL MODIFICATION

As positive feedback continues, the individual begins restructuring their identity and behavior around their online presence. This phase involves:

Increased Time Investment: Hours previously spent in solitary activities or passive consumption are redirected toward content creation, engagement with followers, and platform monitoring.

Identity Fusion: The boundary between the authentic self and the online persona begins blurring. Individuals increasingly see themselves through the lens of their online representation.

Behavioral Adaptation: Real-life experiences are evaluated for their social media potential. Decisions about activities, purchases, and even relationships are influenced by their shareability and likely engagement.

Social Comparison: The individual begins comparing themselves to other content creators, often developing competitive attitudes and envy toward those with larger followings.

3.3 STAGE THREE: EGO INFLATION AND NARCISSISTIC DEVELOPMENT

With sustained validation and growing follower counts, significant personality changes often emerge:

Grandiosity: The individual develops an inflated sense of importance, believing their thoughts and experiences merit broad dissemination and that strangers should be interested in their daily activities.

Entitlement: Expectations develop that others should provide attention, validation, and engagement. Periods without sufficient engagement can trigger disproportionate frustration or anxiety.

Lack of Empathy: As the individual becomes accustomed to asymmetric parasocial relationships where others serve their validation needs, they may lose capacity for reciprocal empathy. Followers become metrics rather than people.

Exploitation: The individual may manipulate followers for engagement, sharing provocative or emotionally manipulative content primarily to generate response rather than authentic communication.

Need for Admiration: The constant requirement for external validation becomes psychologically necessary for maintaining self-esteem, creating dependency.

These characteristics align with the Diagnostic and Statistical Manual of Mental Disorders (DSM-5) criteria for Narcissistic Personality Disorder, though they often represent acquired narcissistic traits rather than a full personality disorder.

3.4 PSYCHOLOGICAL MECHANISMS OF EGO INFLATION

Several psychological processes drive this transformation:

Self-Serving Bias: Individuals attribute positive outcomes (engagement, followers) to their inherent qualities while dismissing negative outcomes (low engagement) as algorithmic failures or audience inadequacy.

Confirmation Bias: Algorithms create filter bubbles where individuals primarily encounter content and perspectives that affirm their existing beliefs, including their positive self-perception.

Availability Heuristic: The constant visibility of validation metrics makes social media success disproportionately salient in self-evaluation, while offline struggles or failures become psychologically minimized.

Dunning-Kruger Effect: Limited expertise combined with positive feedback can create overestimation of one's knowledge and abilities, particularly when echo chambers prevent corrective feedback.

3.5 THE DARK SIDE: WHEN VALIDATION BECOMES VALIDATION-SEEKING EXTREMISM

For some individuals, the pursuit of engagement escalates into increasingly extreme behavior:

Provocateur Transformation: Discovering that controversial, inflammatory, or shocking content generates higher engagement, individuals may abandon authenticity for attention-maximizing strategies.

Moral Disengagement: The dehumanization inherent in viewing followers as metrics facilitates moral disengagement, allowing individuals to justify harmful content if it generates engagement.

Reality Distortion: Living within algorithmic echo chambers and receiving constant validation for increasingly extreme positions can create genuine disconnection from mainstream reality and social norms.

---

4. The Echo Chamber Effect: Reinforcement and Radicalization

4.1 THE ARCHITECTURE OF ALGORITHMIC ECHO CHAMBERS

Social media platforms employ engagement-maximizing algorithms that preferentially surface content likely to generate interaction. Research consistently demonstrates that emotionally charged, controversial, and polarizing content generates higher engagement than nuanced, balanced perspectives.

This creates structural bias toward extremism. Algorithms learn individual preferences and create personalized content feeds that reinforce existing beliefs while filtering out contradictory perspectives. For individuals developing inflated self-concepts and seeking validation, this means:

- Confirmation of their perceived importance and correctness
- Insulation from criticism or alternative viewpoints
- Connection with like-minded individuals who mutually reinforce beliefs
- Progressive normalization of extreme positions

4.2 THE RADICALIZATION PIPELINE: FROM ISOLATION TO EXTREMISM

Radicalization—the process through which individuals adopt extreme political, social, or religious ideologies—follows predictable pathways that social media platforms can accelerate:

Stage 1: Pre-Radicalization Vulnerability

Individuals experiencing social isolation, identity crisis, perceived injustice, or search for meaning represent vulnerable populations. Previously introverted, socially awkward individuals who have experienced marginalization often possess several risk factors:

- Social alienation and resentment
- Search for identity and belonging
- Cognitive openness to alternative narratives
- Technological proficiency enabling deep internet engagement

Stage 2: Self-Identification and Grievance Formation

The individual encounters content that provides explanatory narratives for their negative experiences. This might include:

- Men's rights or incel communities explaining romantic rejection through gender conflict theories
- White supremacist content attributing economic struggles to racial demographics
- Conspiracy theories providing simple explanations for complex social problems
- Extremist religious content offering purpose and community

These narratives are psychologically powerful because they externalize blame, provide identity, and offer community—meeting the exact psychological needs that social media validation addresses.

Stage 3: Indoctrination Through Echo Chamber Immersion

As the individual engages with extremist content, algorithms increasingly surface similar material, creating immersive echo chambers. Within these spaces:

- Extreme positions are normalized through constant exposure
- Group identity develops through shared narratives and in-group/out-group dynamics

- Charismatic leaders or influencers provide parasocial relationships that feel personally meaningful
- Content becomes progressively more extreme as tolerance builds (similar to drug tolerance)

The individual's inflated ego, developed through social media validation, can fuse with extremist ideology. They come to see themselves as warriors for truth, enlightened individuals who see reality clearly while the masses remain blind, or heroes preparing for civilizational conflict.

Stage 4: Jihadization and Action Preparation

The final stage involves preparing for or committing violent action. This is facilitated by:

- Dehumanization of out-groups justified by ideology
- Moral disengagement where violence is reframed as justice, self-defense, or necessity
- Desire for ultimate validation through martyrdom or notoriety
- Parasocial relationships with extremist influencers who encourage action

Significantly, many modern terrorists explicitly seek social media fame, producing manifestos, livestreaming attacks, or creating content designed to inspire copycat actions. Their quest for validation, which began with innocuous social media engagement, culminates in the ultimate attention-seeking act.

4.3 THE INCEL PHENOMENON: A CASE STUDY IN RADICALIZATION

The "involuntary celibate" (incel) community provides a clear illustration of how social isolation, social media dynamics, and radicalization intersect:

Profile: Predominantly young men who experience romantic and sexual rejection, often compounded by social awkwardness or introversion.

Online Community Formation: These individuals congregate in online spaces where they develop elaborate ideological frameworks attributing their rejection to evolutionary psychology, feminism, and superficial mate selection.

Echo Chamber Reinforcement: Within these communities, extreme positions are normalized, including hatred toward women, celebration of violence, and development of fatalistic worldviews.

Ego Dynamics: Paradoxically, while incels express self-hatred regarding physical appearance and social status, many develop intellectual grandiosity, seeing themselves as uniquely perceptive regarding human nature and society.

Pathway to Violence: Multiple mass casualty events have been perpetrated by self-identified incels, including:

- The 2014 Isla Vista killings (Elliot Rodger)

- The 2018 Toronto van attack (Alek Minassian)
- The 2021 Plymouth shooting (Jake Davison)

These individuals followed similar patterns: social isolation, discovery of online incel communities, progressive radicalization within echo chambers, development of grievance-based worldviews, and violent action motivated by desire for retribution and infamy.

4.4 POLITICAL EXTREMISM AND THE LIVESTREAMED ATROCITY

Several high-profile acts of terrorism have explicitly incorporated social media:

The Christchurch Mosque Shootings (2019): The perpetrator livestreamed his attack on Facebook, distributed a manifesto designed for viral spread, and incorporated internet meme culture throughout his planning. His radicalization occurred primarily through online communities, progressing from mainstream conservatism to white supremacist extremism through algorithmic exposure to progressively radical content.

The Buffalo Supermarket Shooting (2022): Similar pattern of online radicalization through extremist forums, production of a manifesto, and attempted livestreaming of violence. The shooter's writings revealed profound social isolation combined with inflated sense of mission derived from extremist ideology.

These cases illustrate how the desire for social validation, initially met through likes and shares, can escalate to seeking notoriety through atrocity. The content creation skills developed through social media engagement are deployed to produce propaganda designed for maximum viral spread.

---

5. Neuropsychological and Psychiatric Dimensions

5.1 DOPAMINERGIC DYSREGULATION AND BEHAVIORAL ADDICTION

Chronic social media use, particularly when reinforced by validation-seeking behavior, creates neuroplastic changes in reward circuitry:

Tolerance Development: Similar to substance addiction, individuals require increasing amounts of validation to achieve the same reward sensation, driving escalating content production and increasingly extreme attention-seeking behavior.

Withdrawal Symptoms: Periods without sufficient engagement produce anxiety, irritability, and mood disturbance, motivating compulsive checking behavior.

Salience Distortion: Social media engagement becomes disproportionately important in motivational hierarchies, displacing other goals and activities.

5.2 COMORBID PSYCHIATRIC CONDITIONS

Several psychiatric conditions show significant association with problematic social media use and radicalization vulnerability:

Depression and Anxiety: Social isolation often co-occurs with mood and anxiety disorders. Social media can provide temporary relief through validation while ultimately exacerbating symptoms through social comparison and disrupted sleep.

Autism Spectrum Disorders: Individuals with autism often prefer online to face-to-face interaction due to reduced social processing demands. This creates vulnerability to excessive online engagement and potential radicalization within narrow interest communities.

Personality Disorders: Narcissistic, borderline, and antisocial personality features show complex relationships with social media use, with platforms potentially exacerbating trait expression.

Psychotic Spectrum Disorders: Individuals experiencing paranoid ideation or developing psychotic disorders may encounter online content that reinforces delusional beliefs, accelerating psychiatric deterioration.

5.3 COGNITIVE DISTORTIONS AND REALITY TESTING IMPAIRMENT

Extended immersion in echo chambers can produce cognitive distortions typically associated with psychiatric pathology:

Paranoid Ideation: Conspiracy theories and extremist narratives often emphasize persecution, surveillance, and malevolent forces, potentially inducing paranoid thinking patterns.

Black-and-White Thinking: Echo chambers discourage nuance, creating dichotomous thinking where complex issues are reduced to good/evil, us/them frameworks.

Grandiose Delusions: Extreme cases may develop genuine delusional beliefs about their importance, mission, or special knowledge.

---

6. Protective Factors and Individual Differences

6.1 WHY NOT EVERYONE TRANSFORMS

Despite widespread social media use, most users do not develop inflated egos or undergo radicalization. Protective factors include:

Secure Attachment: Individuals with healthy early attachment experiences and stable offline relationships are buffered against excessive dependence on online validation.

Critical Thinking Skills: Media literacy and critical thinking provide resilience against algorithmic manipulation and extremist propaganda.

Diverse Social Networks: Maintaining connections across different communities prevents echo chamber immersion and provides reality-testing opportunities.

Emotional Regulation: Capacity to tolerate negative emotions without external soothing reduces vulnerability to validation addiction.

Purpose and Meaning: Individuals with established sense of purpose through work, family, creativity, or service are less susceptible to ideological recruitment.

6.2 DEVELOPMENTAL CONSIDERATIONS

Adolescents and young adults show heightened vulnerability due to:

- Ongoing identity formation
- Neurological immaturity in impulse control and future planning
- Developmental primacy of peer relationships
- Digital nativity and extensive online engagement

---

7. Societal and Cultural Dimensions

7.1 THE ATTENTION ECONOMY AND STRUCTURAL INCENTIVES

Social media platforms operate on advertising-based business models requiring maximum user engagement.

This creates structural incentives toward addictive design, algorithmic extremism, and exploitation of psychological vulnerabilities. The transformation of introverted individuals and radicalization pathways are not accidental byproducts but predictable consequences of engagement-maximizing architecture.

7.2 CULTURAL NARCISSISM AND THE VALIDATION ECONOMY

Contemporary Western culture increasingly valorizes self-promotion, personal branding, and entrepreneurial self-commodification. Traditional virtues of humility, privacy, and self-effacement are devalued in favor of visibility, influence, and audience accumulation. This cultural context normalizes narcissistic traits and validates the transformation process as legitimate self-actualization rather than pathological development.

7.3 LONELINESS EPIDEMIC AND SOCIAL INFRASTRUCTURE DECLINE

Rising rates of loneliness, social isolation, and declining civic participation create populations vulnerable to social media dependency. The collapse of traditional community structures (churches, civic organizations, neighborhood networks) leaves individuals seeking belonging in digital spaces poorly designed to provide authentic connection.

8. Case Studies: The Transformation in Action

8.1 CASE STUDY 1: THE GAMING STREAMER

Background: 19-year-old male, history of social anxiety and difficulty making friends, spent most time gaming alone.

Transformation: Began livestreaming gameplay, developed modest following (5,000 followers) over six months.

Personality Changes: Developed grandiose beliefs about gaming skill and entertainment value, began treating viewers as subordinates expected to donate money, became verbally aggressive toward critics, experienced depression when viewer counts declined.

Outcome: Escalated to creating increasingly provocative content including racist and misogynistic statements to maintain engagement. Eventually banned from platform, experienced identity crisis and depressive episode.

Analysis: Classic pattern of validation dependency, ego inflation, and escalation to maintain dopaminergic reward.

8.2 CASE STUDY 2: THE POLITICAL COMMENTATOR

Background: 24-year-old female, introverted, politically interested but socially marginalized in college.

Transformation: Created social media account sharing political opinions, rapidly gained following (50,000 followers) through provocative takes on controversial issues.

Personality Changes: Developed certainty about political positions despite limited expertise, became dismissive of contrary evidence, experienced relationships ending due to political arguments, began seeing herself as thought leader and future political figure.

Outcome: Continued escalation of extreme positions to maintain growth, eventually embraced conspiracy theories that initially seemed absurd to maintain audience engagement and identity as "truth-teller."

Analysis: Echo chamber reinforcement combined with validation dependency drove progressive radicalization and reality distortion.

8.3 CASE STUDY 3: THE EXTREMIST ATTACKER (COMPOSITE)

Background: Early 20s male, history of social rejection, romantic failure, limited employment, extensive time online.

Transformation: Discovered extremist community providing explanatory narrative for life failures, began creating content within community, developed reputation as ideologically committed member.

Personality Changes: Fused personal identity with extremist ideology, developed grandiose sense of mission, experienced increasing disconnection from family and former friends, came to view violence as justified and necessary.

Outcome: Planned and attempted mass casualty attack, produced manifesto for posthumous social media distribution, sought infamy through atrocity.

Analysis: Complete radicalization pathway from isolation through online community involvement to violence motivated by ideological commitment and desire for ultimate validation through notoriety.

---

9. Intervention and Prevention Strategies

9.1 INDIVIDUAL-LEVEL INTERVENTIONS

Digital Literacy Education: Teaching recognition of algorithmic manipulation, echo chambers, and validation-seeking psychology.

Cognitive-Behavioral Therapy: Addressing negative self-schemas, building offline social skills, developing resilience to rejection.

Mindfulness-Based Interventions: Cultivating awareness of emotional states driving social media use, developing capacity to tolerate discomfort without external validation.

Social Skills Training: Building face-to-face interaction competence to reduce dependence on mediated communication.

9.2 PLATFORM-LEVEL REFORMS

Algorithmic Transparency and Modification: Reducing engagement-maximizing optimization in favor of well-being metrics.

Echo Chamber Disruption: Intentional introduction of diverse perspectives and fact-checking within feeds.

Validation Metric Modification: Reducing salience of likes, followers, and other quantifiable validation measures.

Early Warning Systems: Identifying users showing patterns consistent with radicalization for intervention.

9.3 SOCIETAL-LEVEL APPROACHES

Community Infrastructure Investment: Rebuilding offline social spaces and civic engagement opportunities.

Mental Health Access: Expanding treatment availability for anxiety, depression, and social difficulties.

Media Literacy Integration: Incorporating critical digital literacy throughout educational curricula.

Extremism Prevention Programs: Evidence-based interventions addressing radicalization vulnerability.

---

10. Conclusion

The transformation of introverted, socially awkward individuals through social media validation represents a complex psychological phenomenon rooted in fundamental human needs for belonging and esteem. While social media can provide genuine benefits—connecting isolated individuals, enabling self-expression, and building communities—its current architecture creates systematic risks.

The same mechanisms that enable positive transformation—validation, community formation, identity exploration—can drive pathological outcomes including narcissistic trait development, reality distortion, and radicalization toward extremism. The pathway from initial validation to violent extremism, while traversed by only a small minority, follows predictable patterns that platforms could address through design modifications.

Understanding this phenomenon requires integrating perspectives from social psychology, neuroscience, clinical psychology, and terrorism studies. Intervention must occur at individual, platform, and societal levels, addressing both the supply-side factors (algorithmic design, extremist content) and demand-side vulnerabilities (social isolation, identity crisis, psychiatric conditions).

As digital technology becomes increasingly central to human social life, developing ethical, psychologically informed approaches to platform design represents not merely a commercial consideration but a fundamental public health and safety imperative.

References and Further Reading

ACADEMIC LITERATURE

1. Andreassen, C. S., Pallesen, S., & Griffiths, M. D. (2017). The relationship between addictive use of social media, narcissism, and self-esteem: Findings from a large national survey. *Addictive Behaviors, 64,* 287-293.
2. Brailovskaia, J., & Margraf, J. (2021). The relationship between burden caused by coronavirus (Covid-19), addictive social media use, sense of control and anxiety. *Computers in Human Behavior, 119,* 106720.
3. Bushman, B. J., & Baumeister, R. F. (1998). Threatened egotism, narcissism, self-esteem, and direct and displaced aggression: Does self-love or self-hate lead to violence? *Journal of Personality and Social Psychology, 75*(1), 219-229.
4. Campbell, W. K., & Miller, J. D. (Eds.). (2011). *The handbook of narcissism and narcissistic personality disorder: Theoretical approaches, empirical findings, and treatments.* John Wiley & Sons.
5. Eckhardt, W., & Stivers, R. (2017). The dark side of social media. *Society, 54*(1), 60-67.
6. Gentile, B., Twenge, J. M., Freeman, E. C., & Campbell, W. K. (2012). The effect of social networking websites on positive self-views: An experimental investigation. *Computers in Human Behavior, 28*(5), 1929-1933.
7. Hussain, Z., & Griffiths, M. D. (2018). Problematic social networking site use and comorbid psy-

chiatric disorders: A systematic review of recent large-scale studies. *Frontiers in Psychiatry, 9*, 686.

8. Keipi, T., Näsi, M., Oksanen, A., & Räsänen, P. (2017). *Online hate and harmful content: Cross-national perspectives.* Routledge.
9. Mccauley, C., & Moskalenko, S. (2008). Mechanisms of political radicalization: Pathways toward terrorism. *Terrorism and Political Violence, 20*(3), 415-433.
10. Panek, E. T., Nardis, Y., & Konrath, S. (2013). Mirror or megaphone? How relationships between narcissism and social networking site use differ on Facebook and Twitter. *Computers in Human Behavior, 29*(5), 2004-2012.
11. Ribeiro, M. H., Ottoni, R., West, R., Almeida, V. A., & Meira Jr, W. (2020). Auditing radicalization pathways on YouTube. In *Proceedings of the 2020 conference on fairness, accountability, and transparency* (pp. 131-141).
12. Schmid, A. P. (2013). Radicalisation, de-radicalisation, counter-radicalisation: A conceptual discussion and literature review. *ICCT Research Paper, 97*(1), 22.
13. Twenge, J. M., & Campbell, W. K. (2009). *The narcissism epidemic: Living in the age of entitlement.* Simon and Schuster.
14. Vogel, E. A., Rose, J. P., Roberts, L. R., & Eckles, K. (2014). Social comparison, social media, and self-esteem. *Psychology of Popular Media Culture, 3*(4), 206-222.

15. Winter, C., & Davey, J. (2019). *Radical Gateway or Echo Chamber? The Role of Recommendation Algorithms in Extremist Content Consumption.* Institute for Strategic Dialogue.

REPORTS AND WHITE PAPERS

- Anti-Defamation League. (2021). *Online hate and harassment: The American experience.*
- Counter Extremism Project. (2020). *Livestreaming Terror: The Christchurch Attack.*
- Royal Society for Public Health. (2017). *#StatusOfMind: Social media and young people's mental health and wellbeing.*
- RAND Corporation. (2018). *The Role of Social Media in Radicalization and Terrorism.*

BOOKS FOR GENERAL AUDIENCES

- Lanier, J. (2018). *Ten arguments for deleting your social media accounts right now.* Henry Holt and Company.
- Nagle, A. (2017). *Kill all normies: Online culture wars from 4chan and Tumblr to Trump and the alt-right.* Zero Books.
- Newport, C. (2019). *Digital minimalism: Choosing a focused life in a noisy world.* Penguin.
- Ronson, J. (2015). *So you've been publicly shamed.* Riverhead Books.
- Turkle, S. (2011). *Alone together: Why we expect more from technology and less from each other.* Basic Books.

Appendix A: Warning Signs and Risk Assessment

INDIVIDUAL RISK FACTORS FOR PROBLEMATIC SOCIAL MEDIA USE

- Excessive time investment (>4 hours daily on social platforms)
- Mood disturbance when unable to access platforms
- Neglect of offline relationships and responsibilities
- Progressive isolation from non-online activities
- Identity increasingly defined by online metrics
- Escalating content extremity to maintain engagement
- Defensive or hostile responses to criticism of online behavior

RED FLAGS FOR RADICALIZATION RISK

- Sudden ideological shift toward extremism
- Consumption of extremist content and membership in radical online communities
- Dehumanizing language toward out-groups
- Expressed admiration for violent extremists
- Research into weapons, tactics, or attack planning

- Creation of manifestos or explanatory documents
- Statements indicating intent to commit violence or achieve martyrdom
- Social withdrawal combined with online immersion

ASSESSMENT TOOLS

Professionals assessing individuals should consider:

- Social Media Use Scale: Quantifying time, emotional investment, and functional impairment
- Narcissistic Personality Inventory: Measuring narcissistic trait development
- Radicalization Risk Assessment: Using validated tools like the Violent Extremism Risk Assessment (VERA)
- Social Support Evaluation: Mapping offline relationship quality and quantity
- Psychiatric Screening: Assessing comorbid conditions requiring treatment

Appendix B: Resources for Individuals and Families

FOR INDIVIDUALS CONCERNED ABOUT THEIR SOCIAL MEDIA USE

Support Organizations:

- Internet Addiction Support Groups (various online and in-person options)
- Cognitive Behavioral Therapy providers specializing in behavioral addictions
- Digital wellness apps and programs

Self-Help Strategies:

- Implement platform time limits using built-in tools
- Schedule "digital detox" periods
- Cultivate offline hobbies and relationships
- Practice mindfulness and self-reflection
- Seek authentic connection over validation metrics

FOR FAMILIES CONCERNED ABOUT RADICALIZATION

Resources:

- Life After Hate (organization supporting individuals leaving extremist movements)
- Parents for Peace (support network for families affected by extremism)

- Local counter-extremism programs
- Mental health professionals specializing in radicalization

Warning Sign Recognition:

- Monitor for sudden ideological shifts
- Notice changes in social patterns and isolation
- Observe online activity and community involvement
- Maintain open communication without judgment
- Seek professional assessment if concerned

Report Prepared By: Research Division Bonkers
Date: 2025
Classification: Public Distribution - Educational and Clinical Use

This report is intended for educational, clinical, and policy purposes. It should not be used to stigmatize individuals based on introversion, social media use, or psychiatric conditions. The vast majority of introverted individuals and social media users do not develop problematic narcissistic traits or extremist ideologies. This analysis focuses on understanding risk factors and mechanisms to enable effective prevention and intervention.

www.ingramcontent.com/pod-product-compliance
Lightning Source LLC
LaVergne TN
LVHW022031200926
848481LV00007B/2647
* 9 7 9 8 2 9 5 4 9 4 1 8 5 *